ULTIMATE PLAY-ALONG
DAVE WECKL
LEVEL 1, VOL. 2

Drum Trax

Play-Along for Drums

Project Manager: Ray Brych

Cover Design: Joseph Klucar

Production Coordinator: Hank Fields

WARNER BROS. PUBLICATIONS
Warner Music Group
An AOL Time Warner Company
USA: 15800 NW 48th Avenue, Miami, FL 33014

IMP
INTERNATIONAL MUSIC PUBLICATIONS LIMITED
ENGLAND: GRIFFIN HOUSE,
161 HAMMERSMITH ROAD, LONDON W6 8BS

ACKNOWLEDGEMENTS

Thanks to everyone at DCI Music Video/Manhattan Music Publications and Warner Bros. Publications for promoting the educational side of music and allowing me to participate. Thanks also to the following companies for their continued support: Yamaha Drums, Zildjian Cymbals, Vic Firth Sticks and Accessories, Remo Drum Heads, AKG Microphones, May Microphone mounting systems, Bagend Speakers, and XL Specialty Cases.

CREDITS

MUSIC PRODUCTION	Dave Weckl
RECORDING AND MIXING	Dave Weckl
ALL COMPOSITIONS	John Patitucci, Dave Weckl

MUSICIANS

DRUMS	Dave Weckl
BASS	John Patitucci
GUITAR	Mike Stern
GUITAR MELODY UNISON ON "ROCK"	Andy Georges
PICCOLO BASS ON "REGGAE," "HIP-HOP"	John Patitucci
KEYBOARDS	John Patitucci, Dave Weckl
PROGRAMMING	Dave Weckl
PIANO AND SOLO ON "SHUFFLE"	Otmaro Ruiz

Rhodes solo and comp behind guitar solo on "Straight Eighths;" Rhodes comp on "Hip-Hop" (behind guitar solo); clav comp on "Hip Hop;" Organ comp on "Reggae;" Rhodes comp behind solos and synth solo on "Sixteenth-Note Feel" Jay Oliver.

PRODUCTION

PROJECT COORDINATOR	Rob Wallis
PROJECT EDITOR	Dan Thress
BOOK DESIGN/MUSIC TYPESETTING	Chelsea Music Engraving
COVER PHOTOGRAPHS	Karen Miller

AUDIO MASTERED BY EDDIE SCHREYER
AT FUTURE DISC/LOS ANGELES

CONTENTS

KEY

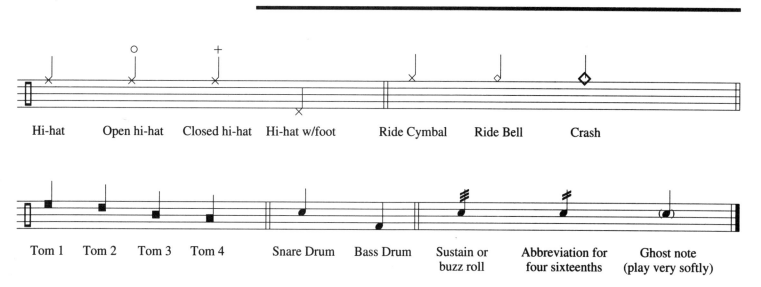

Hi-hat   Open hi-hat   Closed hi-hat   Hi-hat w/foot   Ride Cymbal   Ride Bell   Crash

Tom 1   Tom 2   Tom 3   Tom 4   Snare Drum   Bass Drum   Sustain or buzz roll   Abbreviation for four sixteenths   Ghost note (play very softly)

INTRODUCTION

THE MUSIC

Hi and welcome to Volume II of *The Ultimate Play-Along Series*. This package, like Volume I, is designed for beginner and intermediate drummers with basic reading skills, and for advanced players who want to practice different musical styles along with some great musicians. John Patitucci and Mike Stern (who also have *Ultimate Play-Along* packages available) are featured here on bass and guitar, with Jay Oliver and Otmaro Ruiz on keyboards.

If you are a beginner, I recommend you start with Volume I of this series, which contains more music at different tempos to play along with. Intermediate-level students may start with either Volume I or II. If you are an advanced player looking for challenging material, my *Contemporary Drummer + One* package might be good for you.

Volume I of *The Ultimate Play-Along Series* covered many styles of music, with basic song forms and techniques of working with other musicians and sequencers. In Volume II, we will expand on these ideas, but this time really focusing on the groove and feel. This package features more "live" musicians on the play-along tracks, for a more "human," less rigid feel. The click was played with a cowbell or shaker and has been placed in the background of the mix so as not to interfere with the music, while some of the keyboard comp tracks were quantized to help solidify the overall feel. We all played to the same click and sequence, as you will. The song forms, although simple, contain variations so that your reading, and your decisions about form and interpretation, take on more importance.

One of the essential traits of a good drummer is a good time feel. That's what you should be striving for every time you play. A good time feel also means deciding how you want to present a piece of music rhythmically. So as you work on these songs, really think about how you want them to feel. My tracks are there to show you how I would approach the songs, but don't just copy what I did. Really try to play the tunes your way, with your feel, and most importantly, without overplaying. Remember, these are groove tunes. Practice them that way, experimenting with the subtleties to hear how changing the bass drum pattern or the accents on the hi-hat alters the feel of the song. You'll be surprised how much one little change can affect the whole groove. I will give you a few examples in each song to get you started.

THE CHARTS

Although this package is for beginning and intermediate players, it is recommended that students have a basic understanding of how to read music (notes, rhythms, chord symbols, etc.). Students who play by ear will be able to play along on the strength of their innate talent, but it is still advisable to learn the rudiments of chart reading. There are many ways to write bass parts, and in my experience I've seen everything from chord symbols on scratch paper to very elaborate "miniscores" with piano, bass and drum parts all on one page. However, in Level Two we'll be using a standard format that is common in live and recording situations: a basic chart with some written bass notes, chord symbols, and an occasional piece of additional information. Here is a short dictionary of terms used in written music:

INTRO

The introduction to the song, before the melody or body of the tune.

LETTERS (A, B, C, ETC.)

These serve to identify sections of the song.
Example: **A** melody **B** bridge **C** chorus.

D.C. OR DA CAPO

Go back to the beginning or top of the chart.

D.S. OR DAL SEGNO

Go back to the "sign" 𝄋.

CODA

The end of the piece. The coda is usually played after taking the "D.S." or "D.C." and is indicated by the ⊕ sign. So, for example, if you play through the chart and come to a "D.C. al Coda" marking, you jump back to the top of the chart, and when you come to the measure with the ⊕ sign (usually directly above a bar line), you then jump to the "Coda" (see Straight Eighths chart on page 7).

REPEAT SIGNS ‖: :‖

Play the measures within the repeat signs again, or as many times as indicated.

1ST AND 2ND ENDINGS ⌐1.‾‾‾‾ ⌐2.‾‾‾‾

Sometimes at the end of a repeat sign there will be a first ending, which means go back to the repeat sign and when you get to the first ending measure, skip over it and play the second ending. If there is a repeat sign at the end of the second ending, repeat the section again, skip over the first two endings and play the third ending. If there are no repeat signs in an ending, continue with the chart after playing that ending.

REPEAT MEASURE SIGN ✕

Repeat the preceding measure.

REPEAT MEASURE SIGN ²∕∕.

Repeat the number of preceding measures indicated.

TUTTI

Play as written with the band.

SIMILE

Continue in a similar manner.

sfz OR SFORZANDO

Accent the note very hard, then immediately get very soft.

RITARD

Gradually slow down.

FERMATA ⌢

Hold the note under the fermata (sometimes referred to as the "bird's eye").

CRESCENDO ⟨

Get louder from the beginning to the end of the marking.

DECRESCENDO ⟩

Get softer.

OTHER MARKINGS

♩ Refers to a rhythm without denoting the pitch, unless accompanied by a chord symbol.

\> An accented note.

• A short note.

⌣ Slide up to a note.

pp (pianissimo) Very, very soft.

p (piano) Soft.

mp (mezzo piano) Moderately soft.

mf (mezzo forte) Moderately loud.

f (forte) Loud.

ff (fortissimo) Very loud.

CROSS STICK (SOMETIMES ABBREVIATED CRS. STK.)

Turn the stick around, put your palm down on the snare with the butt end of the stick extending over the rim of the snare, and bring the stick down on the rim. A sort of "wood block" sound is made. You can change this sound by increasing or decreasing the length of the stick extending over the edge.

It is very important to realize that charts are there to inform you as to what is going on with the song. Very rarely will they tell you exactly what to play. You still have to use your ears and play as musically as possible. You don't want to sound like you're reading.

THE BOOK

The book will detail my thoughts on the style of each song, explain some of my grooves, and provide alternate grooves and ideas. I also try, when appropriate, to give some insight into the "roots" of the style and make suggestions for further listening material. Then I "talk down" the chart, going over the basic form and pointing out things to watch for, which is a very common practice at rehearsals and sessions.

SOME THOUGHTS

As a kid practicing drums, I loved to play with records but always wished I could play along without the drums in the mix. My intention with *The Ultimate Play-Along Series* is to provide the kind of material I always dreamed of having, as well as chart reading practice. I believe that, if used as designed, *The Ultimate Play-Along Series* will provide a basis in the skills needed to become not only a good studio musician, but a good musician overall — in addition to being a fun way to practice. I also strongly recommend that students learn basic harmony and piano skills. Future packages will include more "lead sheet"-type charts such as bass, melody, chord changes, etc. Lead sheets allow you to get further "inside" the music and to approach your part from a very musical perspective, if you understand what you are looking at. Learning basic piano and harmony will help you be a more rounded musician, and may even help you become a good songwriter! I know it's hard to take time away from the drums, but even 30 minutes a day devoted to keyboard or guitar will really pay off.

STRAIGHT EIGHTHS

This song has a feel called "straight eighths," rather than classifying it as rock, funk, R & B, etc. I like to let the music, not the chart, dictate what I will play. The chart is a good place to start, but never just assume that what is written is exactly what you should play, unless the composer is adamant about it.

John plays eighth-notes on the bass with an accent on the offbeats almost the whole tune, so really lock in with him and with the "click" (the cowbell on quarter-notes with a two measure count-off). The keyboard part will help you lock in as well. The melody is also eighth-note oriented, but be aware that sometimes a melody instrument may stretch the time and lay back a little, to give it more expression and feel. When this happens, you really have to pay attention to the click and the bass to keep the time solid.

Another thing to think about is the *attitude* with which a feel is conveyed. Even though the dynamic in this particular song is *mf*, the backbeat (snare on 2 and 4) should, in my opinion, still have a "crack" to it. To do this at a medium volume, I hit a *rim shot* (hitting the rim and the head at the same time) on 2 and 4 with a relaxed, easy stroke — not too much arm motion. If you hit the drum with the same velocity, but not as a rim shot, it would sound much softer and would not have the same attitude.

PATTERNS PLAYED/SUGGESTED:

Here are some of the basic patterns and fills I played throughout the song, with a few suggestions for other grooves that might work.

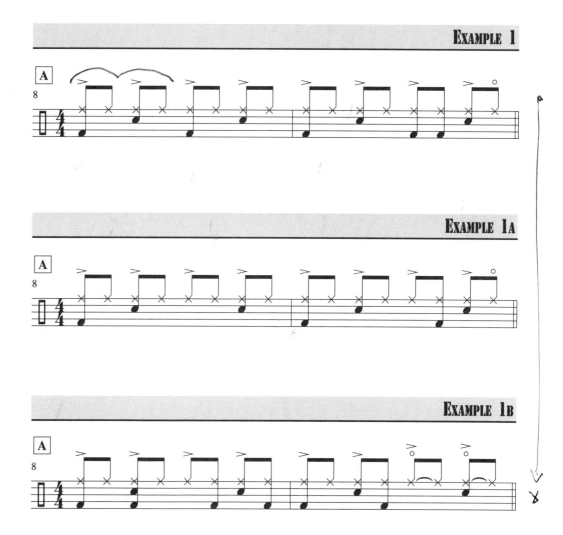

EXAMPLE 1

EXAMPLE 1A

EXAMPLE 1B

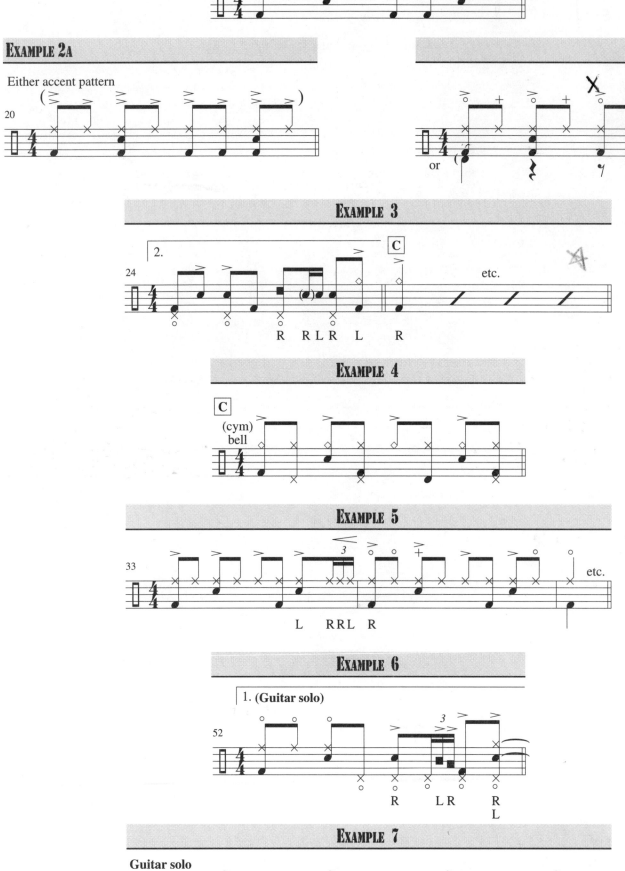

The eight-bar intro starts with the drums and bass and adds the keyboard and guitar at bar 5. At bar 7, a bass line occurs that repeats throughout the song at *turnaround* phrases (every four bars as part of the bass line), which you can either fill around or play time through. Generally a small fill is good when it happens at the end of a phrase, to set up the next section (notice there is no cymbal crash after the fill, though). Although the dynamic is *mf*, this kind of song actually leans toward a more relaxed forte.

The guitar melody starts at letter **A** (bar 9). Go through **A** and **B** again, and take the second ending into **C**. This is the **chorus** of the song. The dynamic marking is *f*, with some keyboard and melody rhythms written. I chose to not pay much attention to the keyboard rhythms, playing them only with the bass drum. At bar 34, there are whole notes in the melody and bass, but the chart says to keep the time going. This means the drums will be the only thing moving here, so I chose to play a repetitive two-bar hi-hat pattern (see Ex. 5) to create a musical hook — something for the listener to latch onto. Your drum groove almost becomes the melody as well as the rhythm in cases like this.

The solo section is at **D**, first for keyboard, then guitar. I always like to treat different solos with different textures and sounds, especially when they are played over the same section. Check out my version, but realize that the next time I play this, it might be different. Don't be afraid to experiment with your own textural approach to the solos. At the end of the guitar solo (bar 70), we go straight to the bass solo for eight bars. The dynamic marking is *mf*, and although you would usually come down in volume for a bass solo, in this kind of song the groove must stay relatively strong, so I took the same approach as in the beginning, a relaxed forte.

At the end of bar 78, we **D.S.** back to the sign at **A**, play through **A** and **B**, and follow the instruction to take the second ending to **C**. Take the **coda** after bar 6; it finishes one chorus phrase. The section at bar 81 is a repeat of the chorus with a first and second ending. As the section builds, I pay more attention to the keyboard figures. The song ends in the second ending with the melody and bass line.

The first thing I always do when I get a chart is scope out the form. I want to make sure I know where to go. A skim might go like this:

The intro is four bars (bass and drums), followed by four more bars with keyboards and guitar.

Letter **A** is eight bars of guitar melody.

Letter **B** is eight bars with a first ending repeat back to letter **A**.

Play through letters **A** and **B**, and take the second ending going to letter **C**.

Letter **C** (the chorus) is an eight bar section with keyboard hits in the background, followed by eight bars of time.

The solo section form is **A**, **B**, **A**, **B**, **C**.

Letter **D** is the same as **A**, bars 46-53 (first ending) are like the **B** section, then repeat back to **D** and take the second ending to the chorus (letter **C**), play sixteen bars, then back to **D** for the next solo using the same form.

After the chorus section the second time, we go on to the bass solo at letter **E** for eight bars. **D.S.** back to letter **A**, take the second ending and go to the **coda** after bar 31.

The chorus feel at bar 81 repeats once, then take the second ending and fine.

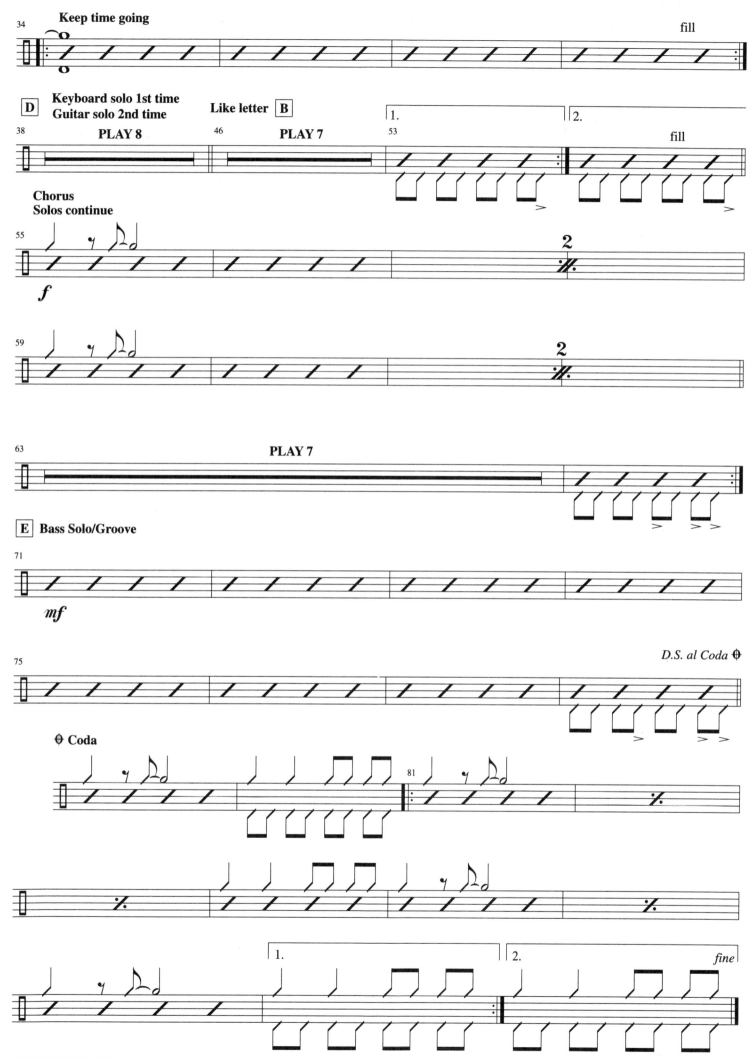

SHUFFLE (BLUES)

Those of you who have worked through Volume I of *The Ultimate Play-Along* will notice that this shuffle is more jazz-influenced than the shuffle in Volume I, because of its "walking" (four quarter-notes to the bar) bass pattern. Here the dynamic starts out at *mf*, and as the solos progress (especially the guitar), the feel gets heavier and starts to rock a little bit.

There are a number of different ways to approach a jazz or shuffle groove, so it is important to get the right feel. On a practical level, because it is easy to under- or over-play the dynamic, simply ask the composer or bandleader how he/she feels it should be interpreted. My rule is, unless the chart says "Loud" or "Rock," I start out quietly so I can build it up later. Keep in mind, though, that a shuffle feel should have an accent on the backbeats (beats 2 and 4) with the snare.

Without going into depth concerning the jazz influence on the shuffle, the concept is based on triplets, and can be thought of as 12/8 rather than 4/4. The best way to familiarize yourself with this important and versatile groove is to go to the source — spend a lot of time listening to and studying the music. Look for recordings with drummers "Philly" Joe Jones (especially John Coltrane's *Blue Trane*) and Elvin Jones. A great reference book for this style is John Riley's *The Art of Bop Drumming* [Manhattan Music Publications, 1995], which provides a good introduction to jazz drumming and an extensive discography of great jazz drummers. And while you're at it, research some of the great blues drummers, whose work has also had a tremendous influence on the music of today.

Of equal importance to the rhythmic foundation of the shuffle is the appropriate sound. Thinner cymbals that sound light and "airy" are preferred. Using rivets (installed by drilling a few holes in the cymbal or by attaching a "sizzle" device that rests on the cymbal) helps sustain the cymbal sound, makes it easier to play the groove, and gives the groove substance without increased volume. If you don't have rivets or sizzles, playing the hi-hats half open creates a similar effect, which is what I used to start this song. I have two sets of hi-hats on my kit. I use the right side hi-hat as my open sound, and I can play 2 and 4, or all four quarter-notes, with my regular hi-hat, using my foot.

There are many options for patterns to play. Here are some I chose, with a few other suggestions:

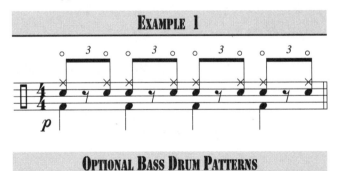

EXAMPLE 1

OPTIONAL BASS DRUM PATTERNS

EXAMPLE 1A

EXAMPLE 1B

EXAMPLE 1C

EXAMPLE 1D

SNARE AND HI-HAT OPTIONS

EXAMPLE 2

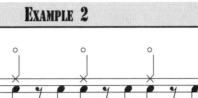

EXAMPLE 2A

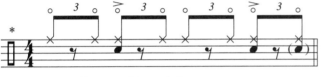

* open or closed hi-hat, or ride cymbal

EXAMPLE 2B

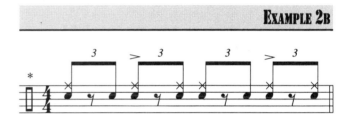

EXAMPLE 3

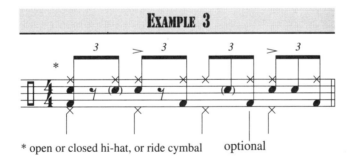

* open or closed hi-hat, or ride cymbal   optional

EXAMPLE 4

Sometimes composers, arrangers or copyists will just write 8th-notes in a swing feel, as you see in the melody parts above the staff in this chart. Usually this indicates that you phrase the eighth-notes as the first and last notes of a triplet, unless it specifies "straight eighths" or unless the tempo is very fast, where the cymbal beat actually "straightens out."

The first measure gives a common shuffle transcription and indicates that the bass part is quarter-notes on all four beats. I choose to play the pattern almost literally, adding accents on the snare and open hi-hat.

When playing the bass drum on all four beats, don't play too loudly. The bass drum should almost be felt and not heard. The dynamic is *mf*, so the whole groove should be approached in a relaxed, light manner. The melody comes in on beat 4, so I give the two swung eighth-notes a little "help," lightly accenting them with the snare and crash cymbal. Be careful not to make too much of melodies written like this. My experience has been that the composer usually prefers the melody to stand alone so that the phrasing can vary. As you can hear, I played time for most of the **A** section (first time through). An approach I sometimes use, as in this case, is to play off of the melody a little more the second time through the repeated **A** (melody) section. This begins in the first ending going back to **A**. Leading into letter **B**, I played a small fill which built up to letter **B**, the "stop time" section. Although it says "stop time," I can usually get away with keeping the hi-hat going on beats 2 and 4. I like to do this because it keeps the feel and prevents the band from losing the time. In fact, unless the bandleader says not to play the hi-hat, I recommend you play it.

In the fourth bar of letter **B** is a common "big band"-type rhythm that the drummer must *set up,* that is, play a fill that will help the rest of the band execute the figure in time and with the right feel. Here the important thing is to play a musical fill. I have what might be called a two-part Philosophy of Fills: first, play something that makes sense with what just happened, and what is about to happen, in the song; second, keep the time and forward motion consistent throughout the fill. In order to accomplish this, I usually keep the hi-hat going, either open or closed, with the foot (as in bar 20), generally playing quarter-notes.

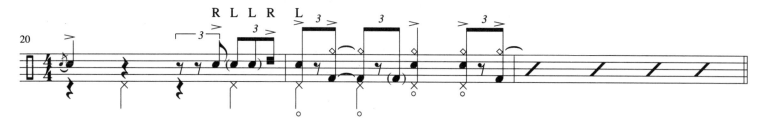

Orchestration is another important aspect of playing rhythms and fills with a band, one which also often comes down to personal choice. To "orchestrate" means to make decisions on which drums to play on, and/or which drum and cymbal combinations you use. My advice is to listen to some of the great big band drummers that were my influences, such as Buddy Rich, Louie Bellson, Mel Lewis, Jack Sperling, and Roy Burns. After the fill, the rest of the melody is played out, with a fill at bar 29 in which I played a buzz roll.

From here the chart tells you nothing but the soloing order and number of choruses for each instrument. Now it's time to use your ears! I like to know which instrument will play first, second, and so on, so that I can select my groove colors (for example, which cymbal I will play) accordingly. During solos, I usually begin softly and build, to give the soloist a relaxed atmosphere in which to create his solo. Use your ears. To begin, I might play a very jazz-oriented shuffle groove on the ride cymbal:

I build a little bit, but as the piano solo is only two choruses long you can't go too far. It's probably better to remain cool with this type of solo, using it as a vamp leading to the guitar solo, which is longer and has time to build. I went back to the open hi-hat to start the guitar solo for a change in color (also because that's what Mike likes to hear behind him) and also give it more of a rock/blues type of shuffle pattern.

I stayed with this for two choruses, then Mike shifted into a distorted sound, so I changed colors as well. Taking dynamics and attitude up a notch, I moved to the ride cymbal and built all the way to the bass solo.

At the bass solo — more precisely, after the downbeat that finishes the guitar solo — the volume drops way down. I find it works better in a jazz-inflected tune to hardly play the bass drum at all at the start of a bass solo. Here again I changed colors, going back to an open hi-hat, playing time and "comping" with the left hand (like a pianist) on the snare drum. When I heard John getting more intense, I followed his lead in order to complement what he was playing. Remember to use your ears and trust your emotions; your instincts, coupled with your experience, will lead you through. That's not a green light to overplay, however.

Coming out of John's solo with a triplet fill that follows his lick, we **D.S.** to letter **B**, the stop time section. Note the choices I made in orchestrating the fills, especially the snare drum in the first fill; the second fill is played more on the toms. Play out the melody, taking the **coda** after bar 26. The **coda** is what's called a *turnaround*, the point at which the chords go back to the four (IV) chord (the last four bars of blues changes) after finishing the 12-bar phrase. The first turnaround comes at bars 45–46, then again at 49–50.

Although each turnaround should be set up, save the bigger set-up fill for bar 48 (I played a big triplet lick) so that the band can easily lock in with that last phrase. Two important downbeats to anchor are at bar 50, which solidifies the melody, and bar 51, because it is written out and sets up the last *tutti* phrase, the phrase which we all play together. Generally it's better to play the rhythm section downbeat than the melody anticipation. I should have played the tutti as a tutti, but instead I let my creative juices get the best of me and played triplets right through the last beat. This is OK, but you should try to play the tutti note for note, since it sounds more appropriate. For the last two bars I played a big flam on the downbeat of bar 52, with bass drum and eighth-notes on the crash cymbals. Notice the *sfz* coming down on the last held note building to the last hit, which I usually play as a few notes rather than just one, in order to give the band a better chance of hitting it together and to add a little more spice to the mix.

THE TALK-DOWN

This is a standard 12-bar blues form that starts with a four-bar intro.

Play letter **A** to the first ending, take the repeat, **A** to the second ending into letter **B**.

Play through letter **B** and into the solo section at letter **C**.

The solo order is: piano (two choruses), guitar (four choruses), and bass (three choruses). After the third bass chorus, **D.S.** back to letter **B**.

Take the **coda** after bar 26 to the fine at bar 53.

SHUFFLE (BLUES)

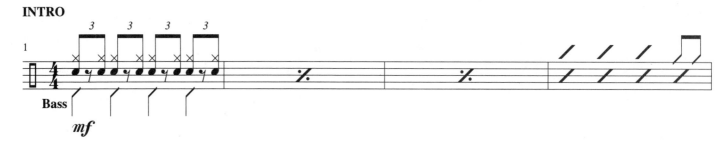

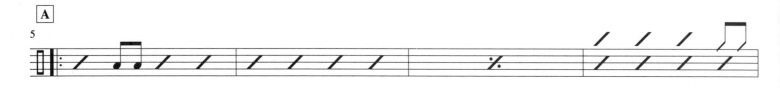

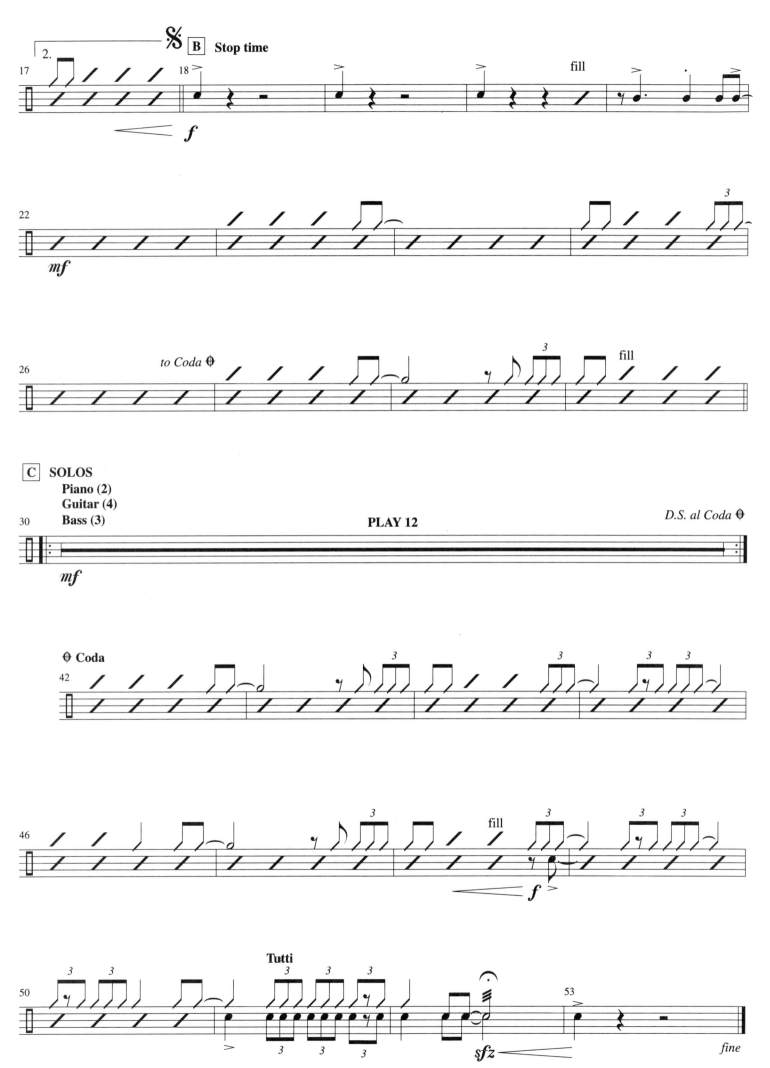

SIXTEENTH-NOTE FEEL

Here is another backbeat-oriented song with a sixteenth-note feel. The first thing you want to know is what the subdivision should be. The way you convey this feeling on the drums will be determined by what the composer, arranger or bandleader wants you to play, what the other musicians are playing, and your own decisions about the attitude, emotions, and feel you want the song to have.

The click for this song is a cowbell on quarter-notes and a shaker on off-beat eighths, with some random broken sixteenth-notes to mimic a real shaker part. The melody, although sixteenth-note-based, will sometimes stretch a little for phrasing purposes. Get used to *not* following those phrasings — the drums need to stay solid and lock in with the click and rhythm section.

THE CHART

Here is another chart that tells you more about what's going on around you than what you actually play. The arranger has decided to give you the basic bass part for most of the tune. But realize that this does not mean you should play every bass note written with your bass drum. This chart lets you know what the bass player is doing, but you must use your ears to find the melody and other rhythm parts that are not written out. My usual approach is to orchestrate some or all of the bass (and other) parts all around the kit, particularly among the snare, bass, hi hat or cymbal.

The intro says this is a sixteenth-note feel, played on the ride cymbal, and the dynamic is $\boldsymbol{f}$. That gives a pretty good idea of how to play the lead-in fill. What I played, starting with the fill bar, is illustrated in Example 1:

EXAMPLE 1

Although the last sixteenth-note in the second bar is tied over to beat 1 (in the chart), I preferred to play both the anticipation (with the snare), and the downbeat of 3 (with the bass drum) in order to keep the pulse of the quarter-note strong, a common move in pop and funk songs. Everyone plays the rhythm at the end of bar 4, which I set up with a small fill on the snare, also playing the last sixteenth-note as a fill leading into the downbeat at **A**. Making the **A** section feel good was tricky: the bass part is rather busy, so I tended to play less, especially on the low (bass drum) end of the kit:

EXAMPLE 2

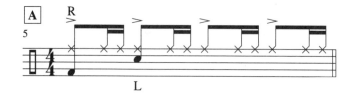

If you are having trouble making a song or groove feel good, *simplify* and *play less!* Such basic streamlining will often bring a groove to life. Check out my approach to the orchestration again in bars 8–9, and which notes I chose to play on the bass drum. The hi-hat part is played with the right hand, and the snare with the left. Also notice how I use the hi-hat to complement the keyboard part in bars 9–12. Try your own ideas as well. Remember, you are *composing* a drum part to fit *with* the music.

The first ending is like the intro, but it didn't feel right to go back to the ride cymbal, so I played straight sixteenth-notes on the hi-hat with two hands alternating, right hand lead, with an accent on the upbeats. The snare drum is played with the right hand.

EXAMPLE 3

I played a similar set-up and fill for the repeat back to letter **A**. The second time through **A** is similar to the first, and in the second ending I played a small fill at the end of bar 17 to set up the quarter-notes in bar 18. Notice that I played eighths on an open hi-hat to help build that measure, then a fill at the end of the bar into the chorus section at letter **B**. This is the same harmonic and rhythmic section as the intro and the vamp, but this time with a melody over it. I chose to play the same groove as in bars 13–16, changing the feel enough without getting too big yet.

After the repeat comes the second ending, and that rhythm sets up a two-bar drum solo/fill around some band hits. My concept here, as usual, was to play something that would sustain the forward motion and feel of the groove.

EXAMPLE 4

For the synth solo I wanted to change the groove and feel, so I played straight sixteenths on the hi-hat with the right hand, accenting each eighth-note.

EXAMPLE 5

In order to play this way, I use a motion called the *Moeller technique:* the wrist moves in a downward motion for the quarter- and eighth-notes, and in an upward motion for the sixteenth-notes in between. Jeff Porcaro used a similar approach on so many of his wonderful recordings, and I've always loved that feel.

The first ending is a kind of sustaining bar for the soloist, and the drums should outline this change in the time feel. Listen to the way I did it. A simple solution would be to play sixteenth-notes on the hi-hat or cymbals (accenting quarter-notes), beats 2 and 4 on the bass drum, and a similar fill going out of bar 34. Use the same approach on the repeat, then fill going into bar 36, letter **B**, and build up to an *f* dynamic. Here again, I wanted to change the feel, so I came up with the following pattern:

EXAMPLE 6

This leads up to a fill into the hits at bar 43, and then into the guitar solo. Remember to make the fill part of the time and groove — keep it going!

During the guitar solo, I wanted to change the texture completely. I opted for the ride cymbal and played more lightly, to create a nice "pad" for the soloist to play over. The first time through letter **D** I played the same broken sixteenth-note part as in the first intro. The second time through I played all sixteenth-notes on the cymbal, picking up the intensity. After the fill in the second ending, I started to incorporate the bell of the cymbal and went back to the driving intro groove for the end of the guitar solo. At the end of bar 60, we **D.S.** to bar 9. Notice the crescendo to the f dynamic on the **D.S.** and take the second ending after bar 12, which builds to the chorus at **B**. Here we play through the first ending, taking the **coda** the second time, back to letter **B**, and then to the **coda** after bar 20. Bars 61 and 62 in the **coda** finish the chorus phrase, and then we're into the vamp, which is like the intro/chorus.

A vamp at the end of a song, especially in a jazz setting, gives the soloist an opportunity to add some improvisational thoughts before the ending. My tactic is just to create a strong time feel and complement the solo instrument (in this case, the guitar) with some accents. The hits in the second ending set up the vamp for the drum solo starting at bar 68. The two-bar vamp repeats four times, totaling eight bars, so treat it as an eight-bar *section* rather than just measure to measure. You also have accents by the band to solo around, so make sure what you are playing works with their hits. Because improvisation is a very distinct statement of one's feelings and one's ability to express those feelings through an instrument, I have decided not to transcribe my solo. It's better that you come up with your own ideas. Start simple, lock with the click, and remember to keep the time feel happening no matter what you play. The band has to understand what you are doing so that they can play those hits together.

THE TALK-DOWN

Fill into the intro, which is four bars.

Letter **A** is an eight-bar phrase into the first ending at 13 for four bars, repeat back to **A**.

Take the second ending into **B**, first ending repeat, second ending into the two drum fill bars 24 and 25.

C is the synth solo over the **A** form, the first ending being an extended phrase (nine bars), repeat, second ending to 36 which is the **B** form for eight bars (two four-bar phrases) into the guitar solo at **D**.

Same form, except eight-bar phrase in first ending this time, repeat, second ending to 53.

The same here as well, the **B** form, two four-bar phrases that **D.S.** to bar 9.

Take the second ending into **B**, first ending repeat, take the **coda** at 21.

61 and 62 finish the phrase, 63 to the first ending repeat, second ending to 68, the drum solo around the hits.

68 and 69 are played four times, ending on the last hits the fourth time.

DAVE WECKL

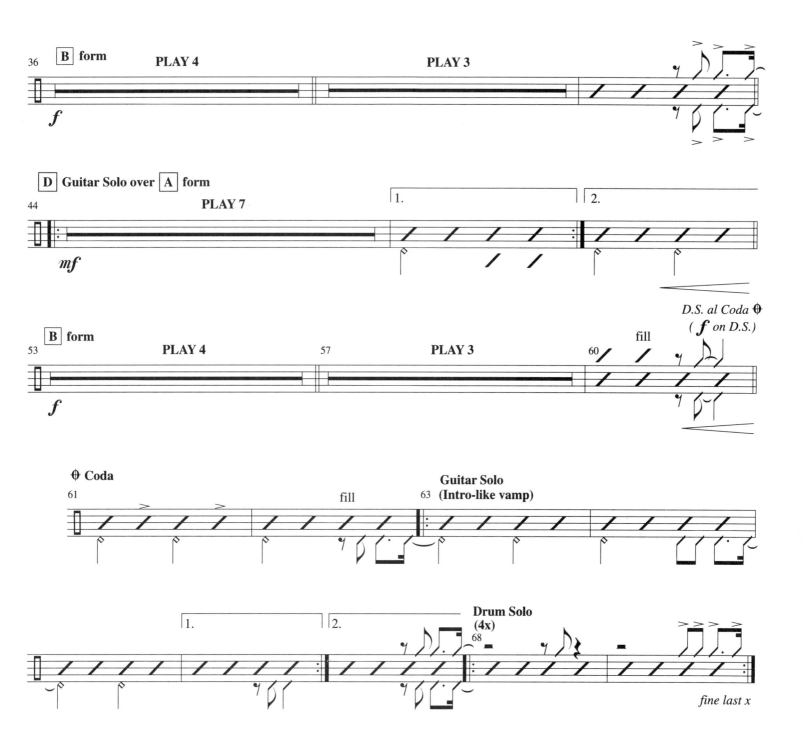

HIP-HOP (JAZZ FUNK)

Hip-hop is a style I am still trying to define. Many of today's hip-hop beats are built on samples of soul and funk grooves from the '60s and '70s. For example, a rap group may sample a few bars of an old Clyde Stubblefield groove from a James Brown record and use it as the basic drum track for an entire song. Though electronic samples and triggered sounds have shaped the sound of hip-hop, some bands are turning to a more live/acoustic approach, with live drums and percussion. Among these bands are the Digable Planets, with Steve Williams on drums, and the Roots, with Ahmir-Khalib Thompson. (If you are interested in knowing more about hip-hop drummers, check out the April '96 issue of *Modern Drummer*.) Here are a few "non-electric" hip-hop beats.

EXAMPLE 1

Digable Planets, "Highing Fly"

EXAMPLE 2

Digable Planets, "Blowing Down"

The third example sounds like a Clyde Stubblefield groove from a record called *Motherload*, by James Brown.

EXAMPLE 3

Digable Planets, "9th Wonders"

The song in this package again comes from more of the style I am comfortable with, which is a jazz/rock fusion context. It has a bit of swing to it, but the straight eighth-note hi-hat part keeps things driving. Opening the hi-hat has become a kind of trademark in hip-hop grooves, commonly on the eighth-note before beat 4, and also at the beginning of the bar. Rather than transcribing what I played, I'd rather you use your ears and just cop the feel. If you really want to get into this type of music, try transcribing some grooves from recordings by James Brown, Sly and the Family Stone, the Meters, the Isley Brothers, Tower of Power, Parliament Funkadelic, etc.

The basic groove I play is not much different than what's written in the first bar of the chart. So lock in with the cowbell click (two-bar count-off) along with the guys and groove!

Although there is no fill marked at the beginning of the song, I played one anyway, partly out of habit and also to anchor the time for the rest of the band and because I think it sounds good in a jazz setting. The basic groove I played is written out in the first measure. I let the sequenced track define the feel for me, which is a common practice on sessions. The chart is fairly simple; the main thing is the feel.

In the intro, I introduced each instrument entrance with a fill. Don't let that become a habit, though, or it will sound predictable. At letter **A**, I left the accents alone in the melody, choosing to save them for later. The **B** section changes harmony so I changed the feel a little, using the hi-hats opening in different spots for variation. Letter **C** is the same as the **A** section melody, but this time I accented the anticipations in the melody (the "and" of beat 4 in bar 37) with my snare and small crash cymbal. Your approach might be just the opposite, accenting the melody in the **A** section and playing time in the **C** section. Leading into letter **D**, hit the accent on the "and" of beat 4 along with the band. The drum solo at letter **D** is a groove solo. Lock in with the tambourine and cowbell for eight bars, then play a fill leading into the guitar solo at letter **E**.

During the guitar solo I wanted to change the groove slightly without disrupting what had come before. I played this section on my right side hi-hat, slightly opened. (Having a second hi-hat on the right side of my kit allows me to really lock in and groove hard.) This eight-bar section repeats four times, so give it some space to build. The first two times through (the first sixteen bars) I played driving, straight eighth-notes on the hi-hat, and on the last sixteen bars of the section I played on the ride cymbal bell, adding accents and building with drum fills around the hits in bar 57. This is the climax of the tune, so my approach was to be a little flashy at first, then bring it back home with the the snare/bass drum/hi-hat in bar 59 to set the band coming back in at letter **G**. This section is the **A** section melody (eight bars) played twice, ending in the eighth bar of the phrase on the "and" of beat four, which I set up with a small fill.

THE TALK-DOWN

The intro is twelve bars long.

The first four bars are drums and guitar.

The second four are with bass.

The last four add the keyboards.

Letter **A** is eight bars of melody and a four-bar vamp.

Play letter **A** twice.

Letter **B** is eight bars long.

Letter **C** is eight bars (letter **A** melody).

Letter **D** is an eight-bar drum "groove" solo.

Letter **D**, the guitar solo, is an eight-bar phrase repeated four times.

Letter **F** is a three-bar drum solo over band hits that acts as a bridge between the guitar solo and the melody.

Letter **G** is the **A** section melody, two eight-bar phrases ending on the "and" of beat 4 in the last bar.

fine

POP BALLAD

In a pop ballad, the dynamic level can get pretty powerful as the song builds. Here the guitar is the melody instrument. Its distorted yet singing tone dictates "big" almost all the way through, but there is still room for dynamic play. After the two-bar count off, the shaker stays in, using the sixteenth-note subdivisions as the click. This opens up several possibilities for playing the song. In the version with drums, I took out the shaker so that it wouldn't obscure my hi-hat part; however, if I know there will be a shaker part in the final mix — an important thing to ask during the session — this will greatly affect what I play, especially on the hi-hat. In my video *Drums & Percussion, Working it Out* [DCI Music Video], I talk about ways of approaching playing with a percussionist. For example, if the shaker is already playing all the sixteenth-notes, there's really no reason for the drummer to do it as well. Normally, I take a "less is more" approach and play a broken sixteenth-note part (as I did here), straight eighths, or even quarter-notes. Practice these variations as well. Here are some examples:

EXAMPLE 1

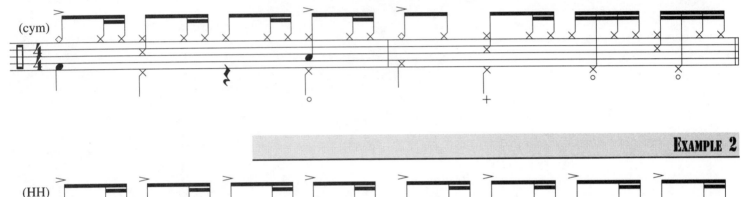

EXAMPLE 2

For this type of song I like to create a big, spacious, very "deliberate" atmosphere with both the time and the fills (studio great J.R. Robinson comes to mind). Remember, your goal should be good, solid time and feel.

THE CHART

The chart for this song doesn't so much tell you what to play as give you an idea of what everyone else is doing. At the top left of the chart, it says "Sixteenth-Note Feel," which is really the most important thing to know. The f dynamic and the keyboard and bass sketches suggest how loudly to play. Essentially, there is a big sustaining chord in the first bar and a rhythmic figure in the second bar, which are then repeated. I began by creating a two-bar phrase to go with what I saw on the chart and what I was hearing from the other musicians, using my ride cymbal, cross-stick, hi-hat and floor tom.

Then I played a big, spacious tom fill (that outlined the theme) leading into letter **A**. At letter **A**, the dynamic level is mf, so I moved to the hi-hat and cross-stick. The abbreviation of four sixteenth-notes is seen in bar 5 (each hi-hat quarter-note has two slashes through the stem). Try using the "shoulder/tip" technique, accenting with the shoulder of your stick on the side of the hi-hat, and playing the unaccented notes with the tip of the stick on top of the cymbals. This way your body motion helps dictate the tempo, rather than it all coming from your head (thinking subdivisions). You might also try some of the other approaches discussed earlier, using eighths and quarters to create a part that complements the shaker track rather than just doubling it.

The first ending (bar 9) is an extension of the normal eight-bar phrase, which I set up with a big downbeat and a fill to match the keyboard part, instead of playing exactly what's written. Letter **A** the second time is similar, but notice where the bass drum is placed in relation to the open hi-hats. The feel is difficult to explain, but what I'm trying to do is create a phrase that complements the music. It again comes down to how to create your drum part to fit the music. The fill in the second ending uses sixteenth-notes to build into the **B** section. Although the **B** section suggests backbeats on 2 and 4, I chose to play the snare on beat 2 and the floor tom on beat 4. Again, it's personal choice. In bar 12 it says "with keys," but be sure to maintain steady time. I find that playing the bass drum on the downbeat of bar 13, after the anticipation in bar 12, keeps the time feel both solid and driving. Also, since the same figure happens again four bars later, I made more of it the second time by using the crash cymbal instead of the hi-hat.

In bar 18 it says "play through," with a whole note written in the bass part. Here I opened my hi-hat, leading to the half-note and the two quarter-notes in bar 19, which I played straight, accenting each note and leaving space. Letter **C** is the chorus and should be one of the biggest sections of the song, especially as you build towards bar 27. I went to the ride cymbal for a big downbeat (after the 2/4 bar), playing the keyboard part with just a crash cymbal, then bringing it down in bar 28 with the ride cymbal only. The hi-hat splashes eighth-notes through the bar to keep the time moving forward. The next four bars are like the intro which sets up the guitar solo at **D**.

The solo section is over the basic form of the song, with the first **A** section a four-bar phrase which I emphasized with a fill and big downbeat. As the drummer, you can take charge in these situations where the form keeps evolving. Do not leave it up to chance — let everyone know, through your fills and phrasing, where the song is headed. The **B** section is approached a little differently, with a cross stick on 2 and a snare on 4 instead of a floor tom. This time I played time, and a fill, at bar 49 going into the chorus section.

Notice the fill at bar 53. It's a big fill, but the time is kept by the eighth-notes on the hi-hat (with the foot), and the snare drum backbeat stays consistent on beat 4 as part of the fill.

EXAMPLE 3

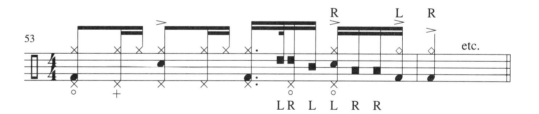

From here on out, the song keeps building. I played crashes every two beats through the 2/4 bar, then I played crash cymbals along with the keyboard part (still keeping the backbeats going!) in the final two bars of the guitar solo at bars 57 and 58. This is the climax of the song, so the intensity should be at its greatest in these two bars, releasing with the fill into the final two-bar intro section. In the final **A** section, the melody repeats over four bars the first time and five bars the second (the opposite of the way it occurred at the top of the song), so outline it appropriately. The dynamic level builds slightly in bars 65–66, then comes back down in the two-bar vamp, ending at bar 69.

Intro for four bars.

Letter **A** to the first ending (five-bar phrase).

Repeat letter **A** and go to the second ending (four-bar phrase) into letter **B**.

Letter **B** is a nine-bar phrase leading into the chorus at letter **C**.

Letter **C** is also a nine-bar phrase, with a 2/4 bar at measure 26.

At measure 29 there's a four-bar "Intro-like" interlude before the guitar solo at **D**.

The solo section is over the form of the song **A**, **A**, **B**, **C** building all the way to measure 59, the intro section (two bars this time), before the last **A** section.

In the last **A** section, take all the endings (first, second, third, fourth) ending in the fourth ending.

POP BALLAD

INTRO

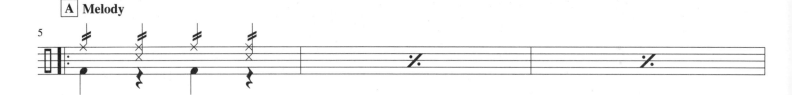

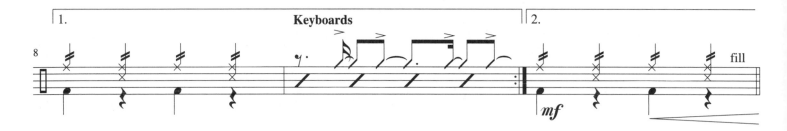

REGGAE (SHUFFLE STYLE)

This style of music, originating in Jamaica, has a wonderful feel and a lot of history. As with any style, the more you learn about its culture — the more you'll learn about its music.

Most of what I know about reggae comes from the drumming of Sly Dunbar, who, along with the bassist Robbie Shakespear, formed one of Jamaica's most popular rhythm sections and can be heard on numerous records including most of those from Peter Tosh. I've also listened to Bob Marley and the Wailers records with Aston and Carlton Barrett on bass and drums. Jamaican percussionist Larry McDonald, who has played with the Skatalites, Rastesfa and Gil Scott-Heron, and is very knowledgeable on reggae drumming, has also given me insight into reggae grooves and the music generally. Larry feels that everything that comes under the umbrella term "reggae" is basically a variation of one of three related musical styles: Reggae, Rock Steady, and Ska.

I suggest you listen to some authentic reggae recordings. In addition to Marley and Tosh, some of the originators include Lloyd Knibb, Theophilus Beckford, Laurel Aiken, Winston Grennan, Amos Milburn, and Alton Ellis. A more in-depth study would be to get a compilation-collection put out by some of the record companies. One I recommend is *The Island Collection, Tougher Than Tough*.

The grooves on this song derive from a "shuffle-ska" feel, which is my interpretation of these authentic Jamaican beats, with a nod to drummer Stewart Copeland of the Police. This is simply how I might approach a reggae tune. My experience is that, at least from a drummer's perspective, pure reggae grooves are straighter, with the guitars floating between a straight and a swing feel. Here are a couple of standard reggae-type grooves:

EXAMPLE 1

Basic ska rhythm from Lloyd Knibb of the Skatalites

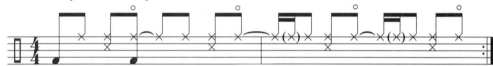

EXAMPLE 2

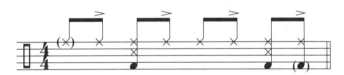

EXAMPLE 3

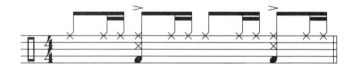

EXAMPLE 4

Sly Dunbar groove from "Sly, Wicked and Slick"

EXAMPLE 5

EXAMPLE 6

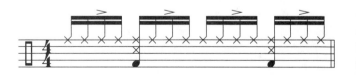

THE CHART

The hardest thing about this chart is the way it is written. These examples and the chart are written in a half-time pulse, so the subdivision is sixteenth-notes instead of eighth-notes, and the upbeat keyboard falls on the "ands" of the beat (composers or arrangers may notate this differently on sessions). Remember, this is a shuffle reggae feel, so all sixteenth-notes are swung unless otherwise indicated. A good way to keep the time straight with the notes you are reading is by counting "1 and 2 and 3 and 4 and" as soon as you hear the cross-stick and shaker eighth-note count offs. Keep counting until you get used to hearing the song and looking at the chart this way. The rhythm notation in the first bar and the indication "shuffle feel" is a good guide to what the composer has in mind. Given this information, I chose to play the following groove:

EXAMPLE 1

Here is a more basic, but still appropriate, groove that you may want to start with.

EXAMPLE 2

The dynamic is *mf*, so approach this groove with a lighter touch. The melody begins at letter **A** and gives you a few hints as to where the phrases are. A common move in reggae is to accent the beginning of a phrase with a rim shot played on the downbeat. I used this idea in bars 7 and 8 along with the melody. You can also add a cymbal bell to the rim shot, which I did later in the guitar solo. Another idea is to straighten out the sixteenth-notes, as I did on the hi-hat in measure 10 the second time through. The melody anticipates the downbeat in this bar, so I played that phrase a little bit differently each time. Again, a lot of my ideas come from my background in jazz and improvisation, which stresses filling in holes where a percussionist might normally play. If there were a percussionist on this track, I would probably play a simpler beat with fewer fills.

At letter **B**, the bass and melody line suggests a different feel, but I kept the drums moving in the same direction as before, with an eighth-note pulse and "drop" (the bass drum backbeat pulse) on beats 2 and 4. The groove that I play in this section, at letter **B**, is one that I use a lot, even in funk tunes, to break up the beat into a half-time feel. Here is Stewart Copeland's influence coming through again. This groove is also played at letter **C** and looks something like this:

EXAMPLE 3

Here is a more basic version of the same thing. Remember to swing the sixteenth-notes in both of these examples.

EXAMPLE 4

One reason I chose to play this groove with the eighth-note bass drum pattern is because there is no bass line — the bass is playing along with the melody. Used in this fashion, the bass drum puts down a nice bottom that otherwise would not be in the music.

Since I knew that this section ends the tune, I wanted to save a little energy for the end, so I stayed on the hi-hat, filling in a few holes and accenting the melody here and there. The guitar solo at letter **D** starts with an *mf* dynamic, and the form is **A–B** played twice. The dynamic level goes up to *f* the second time, so I changed the groove to an eighth-note feel on the bass drum, along with the ride cymbal and hi-hat. The basic groove is as follows:

EXAMPLE 5

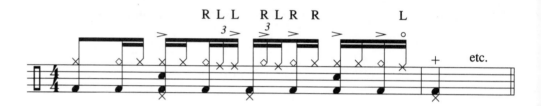

The guitar keeps building through the **B** section again, then a two-bar drum break (remember, the slower pulse feels like four bars at the faster tempo). Give yourself a point of reference by playing eighth-notes on the hi-hat with your foot. Whenever you solo, whether it's two bars or twenty, try to think about form. Each solo should have a beginning, a middle and an end.

At the end of the drum solo we take the **D.S.** back to letter **A**, and it's a good idea to accent the downbeat, clearly delineating the form. Don't take the repeat at the end of letter **B**, and go straight to letter **C**. Because this is the last eight bars of the tune, I used the ride cymbal this time to increase the intensity level. I also played a few more accents in the melody, especially in the last two bars.

THE TALK-DOWN

Play a one-beat fill leading into the four-bar intro.

Letter **A**, the melody, is eight bars long.

Letter **B** is four bars, with a repeat back to **A**.

Play **A–B**, then on to letter **C**, the unison section.

Letter **C** is eight bars long leading to the guitar solo.

The guitar solo section, letter **D**, is played over the **A–B** form played twice (two choruses).

After the guitar solo there is a two-bar drum break that sets up the **D.S.** back to letter **A**.

Play letter **A**, then **B** (no repeat), and then letter **C**.

The fine is the last bar of the **C** section.

This song is just a loud, bashing good ole' rock 'n' roll tune. There are basically two dynamic levels in songs like this: loud and louder. The thing to try and avoid is to overplay. If you hold your sticks loosely, with your hands relaxed, they will be able to rebound off the drums and draw the sound out, rather than trying to muscle it out, and you'll get a bigger sound. Try a little test: grip the sticks tightly and hit them together. Now hold them loosely and hit them together. Notice how open and resonant the sound is as opposed to the closed, choked sound the tighter grip produced? Same thing applies to the drums. My current teacher, Freddy Gruber, calls this the "Action-Reaction" principle.

The groove to this tune is very eighth-note oriented, with the bass and/or guitar playing eighth-notes most of the time. Really listen to the other guys and lock in with their phrasing as well as with the quarter-note cowbell click.

EXAMPLE 1

Opening fill

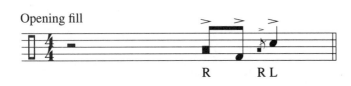

EXAMPLE 2

Main groove

EXAMPLE A

Optional hi-hat patterns with the foot

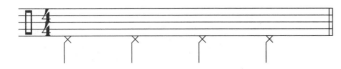

EXAMPLE B

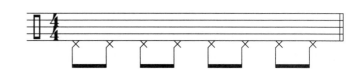

EXAMPLE C

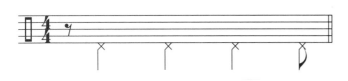

EXAMPLE D

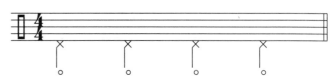

EXAMPLE 3

optional cymbal

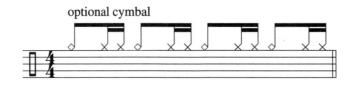

THE CHART

The chart, once again, says nothing about what you are to play, but tells you what's going on around you. The feel, "Straight 8th-note Rock," is written at the top. That's the first thing you need to know. The dynamic is f, so play loud and strong but don't overplay. For this song, you need a nice loud bell on your ride cymbal. Although there are a lot of eighth-note anticipations (on the "and" of beat 4), I chose not to play very many of them, and when I did, I played both the anticipation and the downbeat of the next bar. This keeps the time moving forward. In the first ending there is a four-bar drum break. Notice how I approached this break with a combination of time and fills, avoided playing the downbeat of every bar, and kept my hi-hat splashing on quarter-notes.

At letter **B**, the guitar and bass split up from their unison melody (the guitar is written above the staff, the bass in straight eighths below). I didn't change the bass drum and snare pattern too much; here, the color change comes from opening the hi-hat. I played straight eighths on the hi-hat, but another suggestion would be loud and ringing quarter-notes (which I played in bars 23 and 24), letting the bass carry the eighth-note motion. At bar 20, there is a line played by both the guitar and bass that recurs throughout the song, and in this case is part of the melody leading into letter **C**. Again I chose to play both the anticipation and the downbeat into **C**. Also, this being the first time through this section, I didn't hit many of the other hits, opting to save some for later (skimming the chart showed me that this section happens more than once). I wanted to have somewhere to go in the song, not give everything away the first time through.

I played a simple eighth-note fill going into the guitar solo at letter **D**. At **D**, it seemed a change in feel was in order, so I used an eighth-note pattern on my closed (though not too tight) hi-hat. I still wanted it to sound loose and raw — too tight wouldn't have the right attitude. I wanted to keep solid time through this section, identify the eight-bar phrases with small fills, and complement the solo with a few accents (like playing the snare on beat one). At bar 45, the guitar plays over the **C** section of the song. I opened up the hi-hat a bit, kept hitting downbeats through the anticipations the bass is playing, and then played a big fill leading into bar 49. This section is sixteen bars of the letter **D** groove, so I took it up a notch and moved to the ride cymbal. Bar 57 starts another eight-bar phrase, which ends with the unison line going into another **C** section with a first and second ending. In the second ending, I played a big fill using sixteenth-notes on the snare starting on beat 4, then taking the **D.S.** back to letter **A**.

Since I was on the ride cymbal at the end of the guitar solo, I changed the color of the **A** section with an open hi-hat. The second time through **A**, I went back to the cymbal bell to build it, and then back to the open hi-hat for the **B** section at the second ending. The guitars start to play around the melody a little, so I did the same, adding a few more snare and cymbal accents. At letter **C** this time, I started to pay a little more attention to the bass accents with my bass drum. At the **coda**, I played a big fill into bar 71, played that measure *tutti* with everyone else, then used a big sixteenth-note fill to end the song on the "and" of beat 4 in bar 72. Here I ended with just the cymbal crash, letting it ring out. Had this been a live situation, I would have filled the final whole note with either a big cymbal roll or solo-oriented fills, and then ended together with the band on the downbeat. So feel free to go for it at the end and wrap it up by the last guitar slide. Have fun!

THE TALK-DOWN

Play a two-beat fill leading into letter **A**.

Letter **A** (first time) is eight bars plus four bars of solo drums (the first ending).

Letter **A** (second time) is eight bars, then letter **B** (the second ending).

Letter **B** is eight bars leading to letter **C**.

Letter **C** is a repetitive four-bar phrase played twice that acts as a bridge to the guitar solo.

The guitar solo (starting at letter **D**) is sixteen bars (**A** groove), eight bars (**C** groove), 24 bars (**D** groove), eight bars (**C** groove).

At the end of the guitar solo, **D.S.** back to letter **A**.

Take both endings of letter **A**, play through letter **B**, take the **coda** at the end of the seventh bar of **C**.

The **coda** is four bars long, ending with a unison line on the "and" of beat 4 in the third bar.

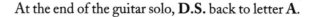

ROCK

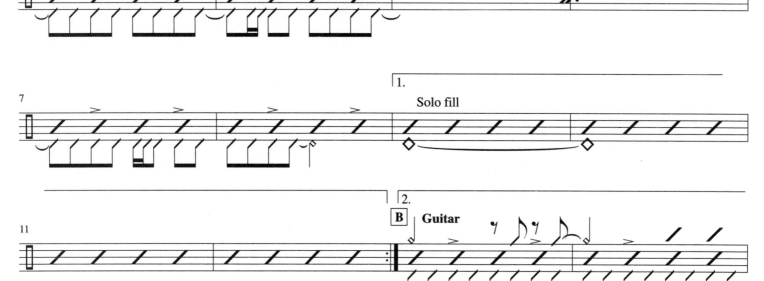

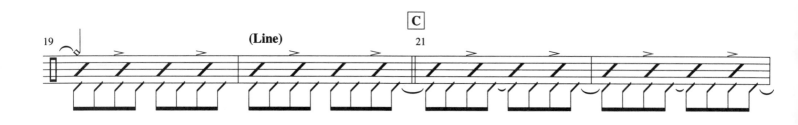

DAVE WECKL

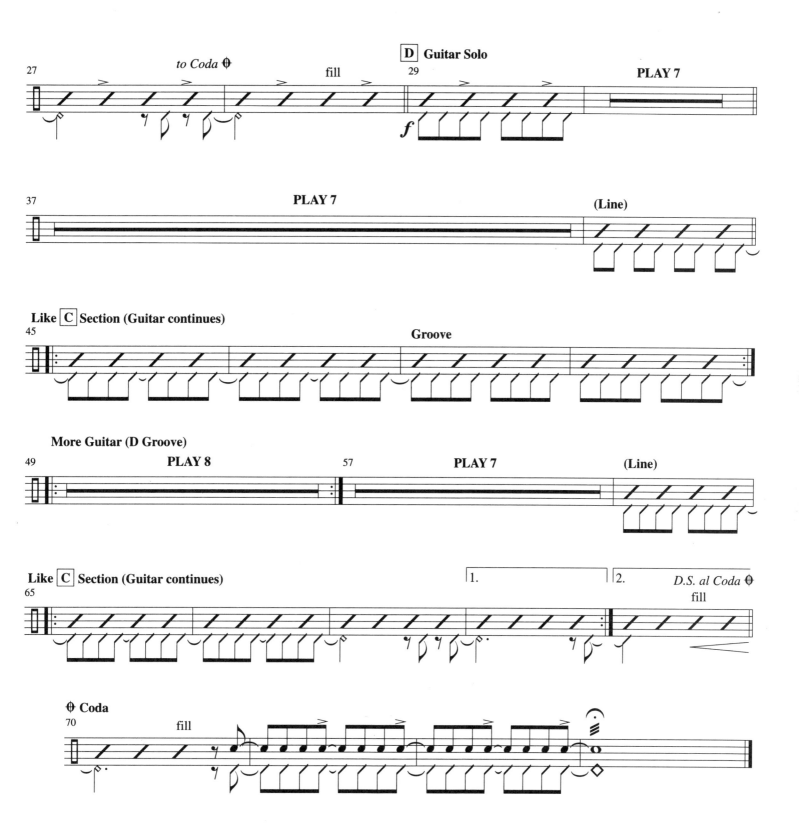

ALSO AVAILABLE FROM MANHATTAN MUSIC

Books/Audio

KENNY ARONOFF • Power Workout 1* • Power Workout 2*
GREGG BISSONETTE • Private Lesson* • Playing, Reading, and Soloing with a Band*
DENNIS CHAMBERS • Serious Moves* • In The Pocket*
LIBERTY DEVITTO • Off The Record
ANTON FIG • In The Groove
DUDUKA DA FONSECA AND BOB WEINER • Brazilian Rhythms For Drumset
STEVE GADD • Up Close*
LINCOLN GOINES AND ROBBY AMEEN • Funkifying The Clave: Afro-Cuban Grooves For Bass and Drums
MICHAEL LAUREN • Understanding Rhythm
LESSONS WITH THE GREATS VOL. 1 • Aronoff, Bissonette, Bozzio, Erskine, Smith, Weckl, and Xepoleas
LESSONS WITH THE GREATS VOL. 2 • Alenander, Moffett, Peart, Kennedy, Parker, Portnoy, and Xepoleas
FRANK MALABE AND BOB WEINER • Afro-Cuban Rhythms For Drumset
SIMON PHILLIPS • Simon Phillips*
KIM PLAINFIELD • Advanced Concepts
JOHN RILEY • The Art Of Bop Drumming
DAVE WECKL • Contemporary Drummer + One • Back To Basics* • The Next Step*
• Ultimate Play-Along For Drums Level One

*Video Transcription Series

Videos

ALEX ACUNA • Drums and Percussion
KENNY ARONOFF • Laying It Down • Power Workout 1 • Power Workout 2
GREGG BISSONETTE • Private Lesson • Playing, Reading, and Soloing with a Band
TERRY BOZZIO • Solo Drums
CLAYTON CAMERON • The Living Art Of Brushes
DENNIS CHAMBERS • Serious Moves • In The Pocket
BILLY COBHAM • Drums By Design
PETER ERSKINE • Everything Is Timekeeping • Timekeeping 2
STEVE GADD • Up Close • In Session
OMAR HAKIM • Express Yourself
GENE KRUPA • Jazz Legend
ROD MORGENSTEIN • Putting It All Together

NEW ORLEANS DRUMMING:
HERLIN RILEY Ragtime and Beyond • **JOHNNY VIDACOVICH** Street Beats-Modern Applications

BUDDY RICH MEMORIAL CONCERT:
TAPE I Featuring Louie Bellson, Gregg Bissonette, and Dennis Chambers
TAPE II Featuring Vinnie Colaiuta, Steve Gadd, and Dave Weckl
TAPE III Featuring Neil Peart, Marvin "Smitty" Smith, and Steve Smith
TAPE IV Featuring Omar Hakim, William Calhoun, and Neil Peart
SIMON PHILLIPS • Simon Phillips • Simon Phillips Returns
CHAD SMITH • Red Hot Rhythm Method
STEVE SMITH • Part One • Part Two
DAVE WECKL • Back To Basics • The Next Step
DAVE WECKL AND WALFREDO REYES, SR. • Drums and Percussion–Working It Out 1 • Working It Out 2

**FOR A COMPLETE CATALOG OF MANHATTAN MUSIC, DCI MUSIC VIDEO, AND REH VIDEO PRODUCTS, CONTACT
WARNER BROS. PUBLICATIONS 15800 N.W. 48TH AVENUE MIAMI, FL 33014 (800) 628-1528 (305) 620-1500**

THE FOLLOWING PAGES HAVE BEEN PERFORATED SO THAT THEY CAN BE REMOVED AND PLACED ON A MUSIC STAND

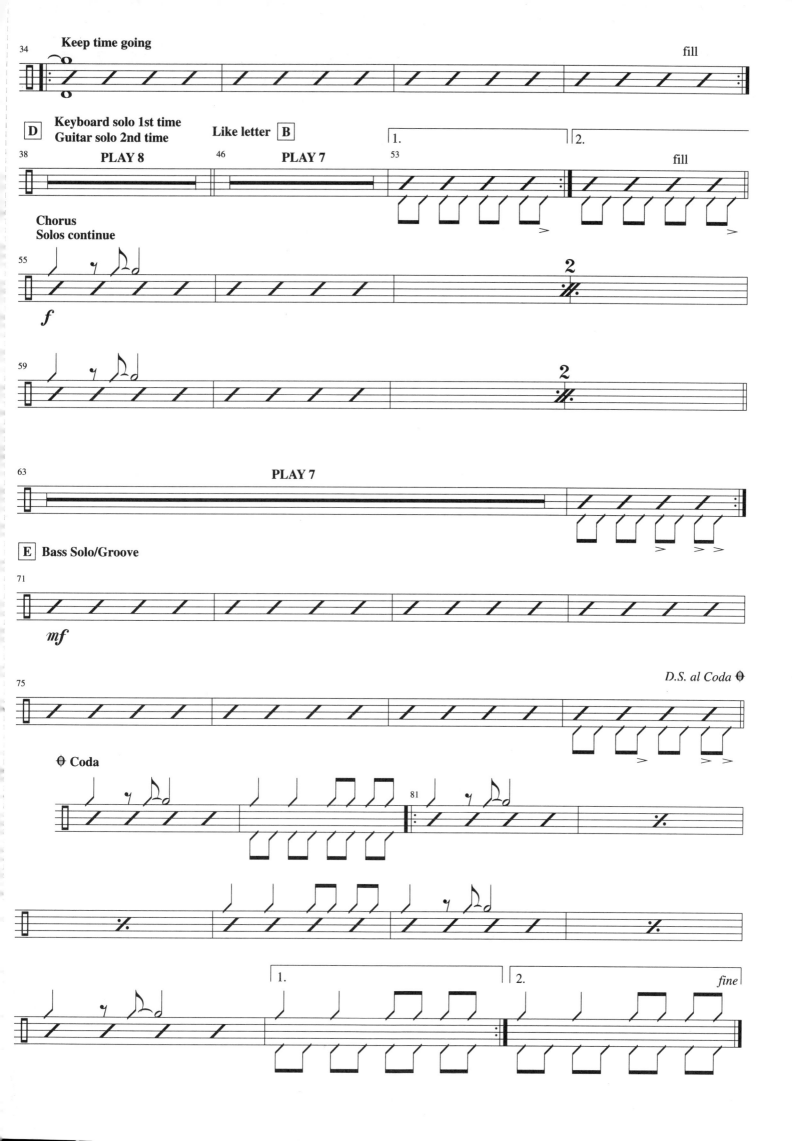

SHUFFLE (BLUES)

INTRO

A

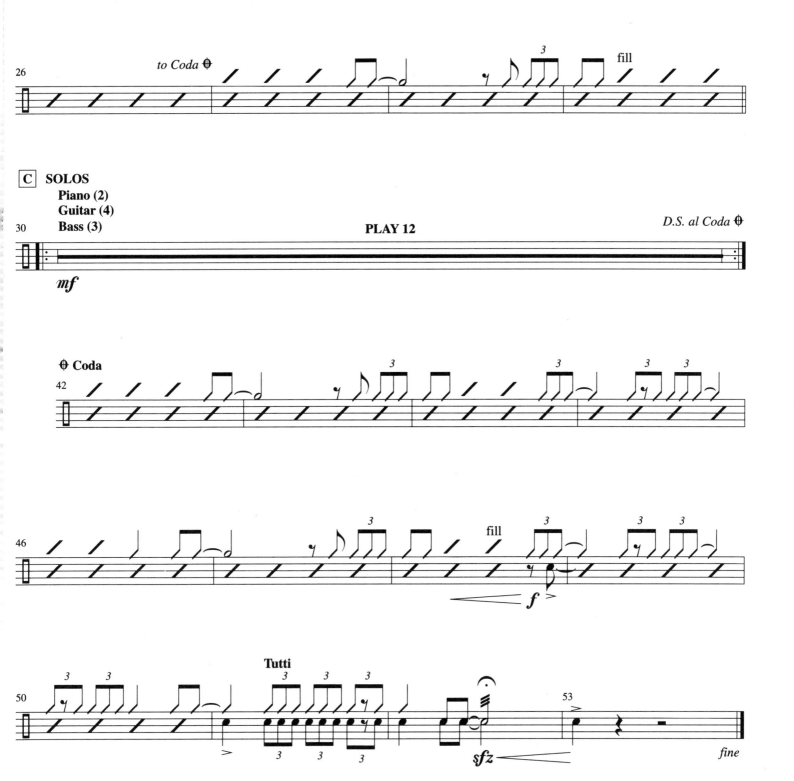

SIXTEENTH-NOTE FEEL

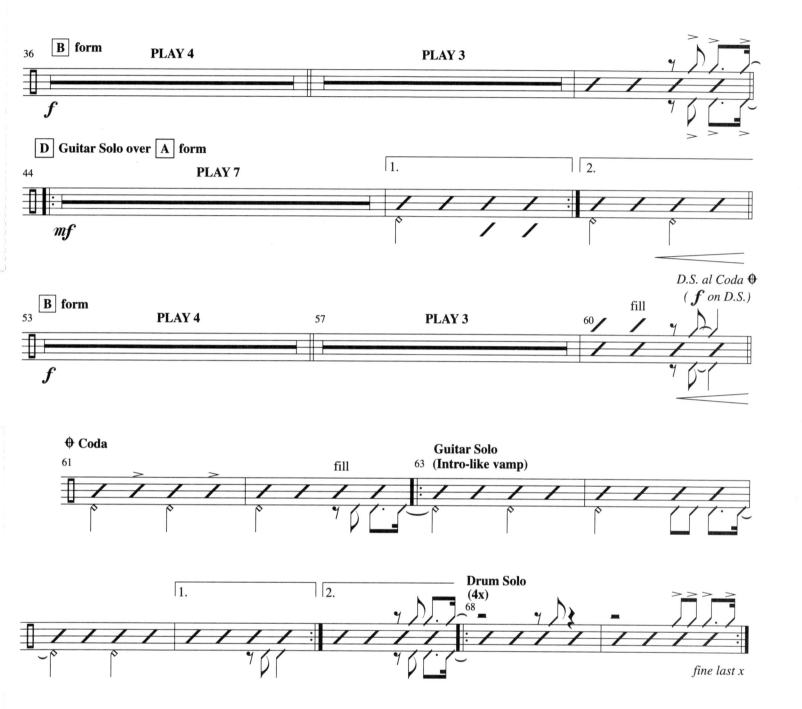

HIP-HOP (JAZZ FUNK)

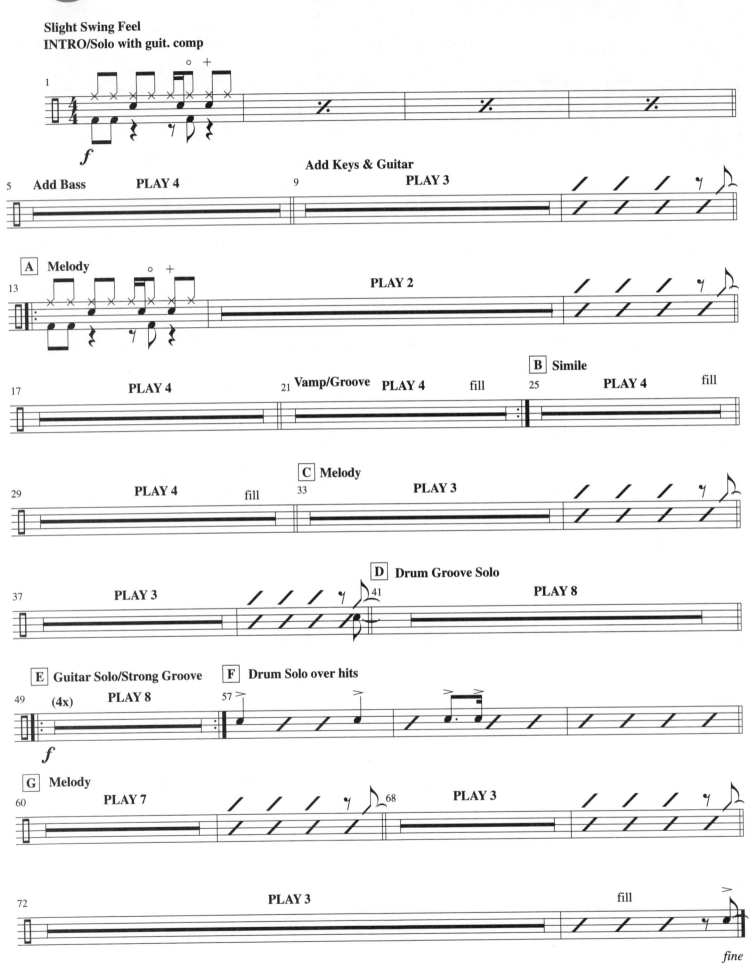

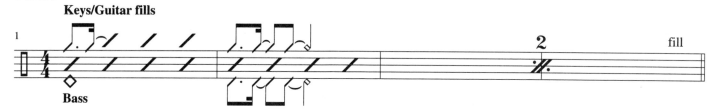

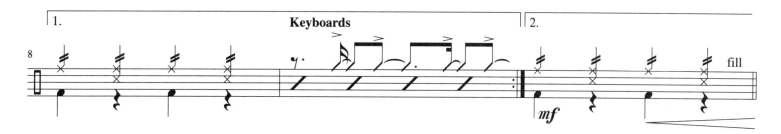

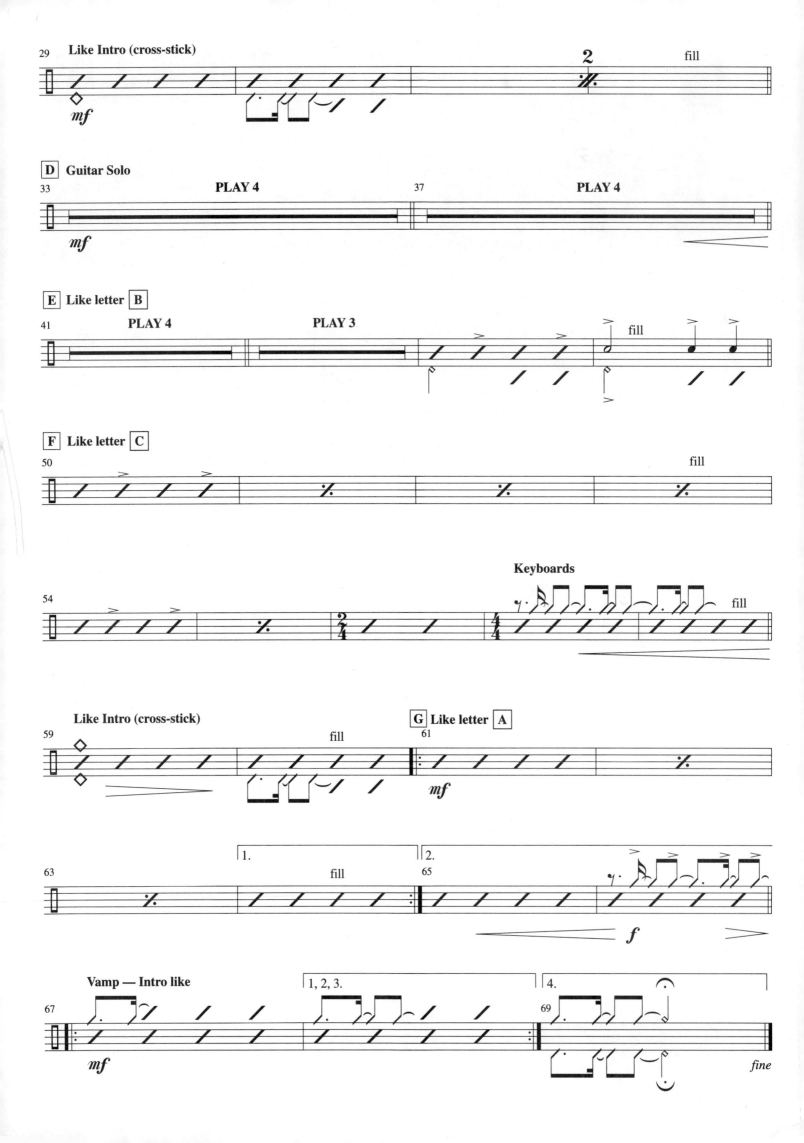

REGGAE (SHUFFLE STYLE)

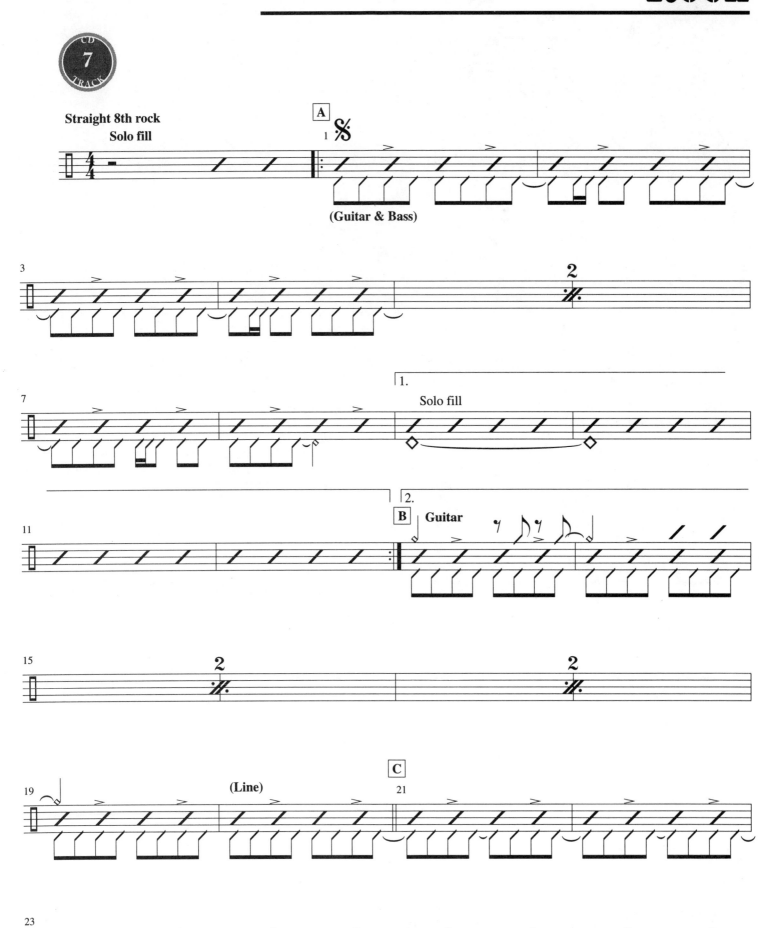

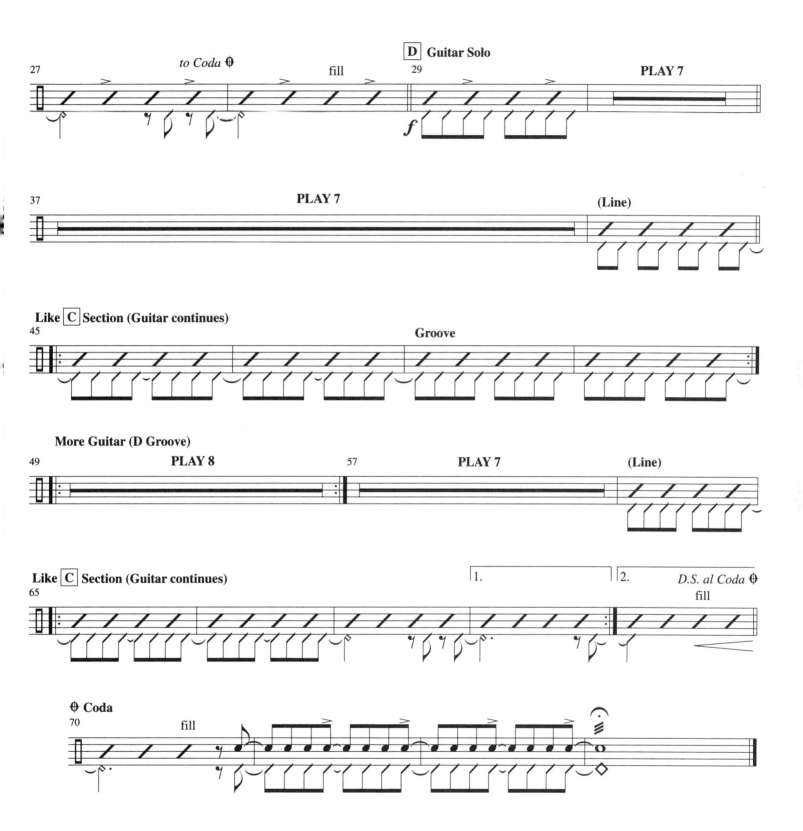

THE DRUMSET SOLOIST

by Steve Houghton

(EL9602CD)
Book and CD

Soloing is often neglected in the drumset player's routine. **The Drumset Soloist** was written to provide you with the practice material to approach any drumset solo, in any style, with ease.

You will quickly build the vocabulary and confidence in soloing as the book progresses through many musical styles. Techniques such as trading, playing over vamps and playing over kicks (or figures) are examined, demonstrated and made available in a play-along format. This allows you to study the style, hear the style, and then practice soloing over the style with a real band.

This book will challenge, inspire and, most of all, let you create and improvise without the pressure of a live gig.

PERCUSSION PRODUCT FROM

(MMBK0048AT) w/Cass.
(MMBK0048CD) w/CD

(MMBK0040AT) w/Cass.
(MMBK0040CD) w/CD

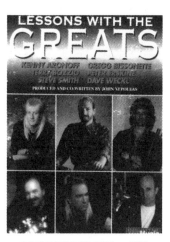

(MMBK0017CD) w/CD

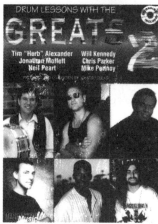

(MMBK0062CD) w/two CDs

(EL03692AT) w/Cass.
(EL03692CD) w/CD
(Spanish & English text)

(MMBK0059AT) w/Cass.
(MMBK0059CD) w/CD

(MMBK0004CD) w/CD
(Spanish & English text)

(MMBK0057CD) w/CD

(MMBK0001AT) w/Cass.
(MMBK0001CD) w/CD

(MMBK0009AT) w/Cass.
(MMBK0009CD) w/two CDs

(MMBK0056CD) w/CD

(MMBK0043CD) w/CD

Produced by Manhattan Music Publications